God's Leading

R.E. Clark

GnG Publishers
122 Skinner St.
Centerton, AR 72719

First Edition
Published by GnG Publishers
8/9/2013

Printed in the United State of America
Cover photo courtesy: StockPhotosforFree.com
ISBN-13: 978-0615864723
ISBN-10: 0615864724

DEDICATION

To my wife, Trudy, who has encouraged me to place my thoughts on paper and into e-book form with the hope that many will come to know JESUS.

Table of Contents

ACKNOWLEDGMENTS

So many have been instrumental in the writing of this book that it would take another book just to list them all. Interestingly, most of them do not know that they have played such a part in my life. They walked along side me as I preached the Word of God. Out of those years of preaching and having congregations that supported my ministry, I have come to realize that there are few if any sermons that should be preached only once.

Thanks to all of you that have been dear friends and encouragers along the way.

Once again, I am grateful to my administrative assistant, who just happens to be my daughter, and my wife. They have faithfully helped me again in proofreading and giving honest feedback in the writing of this book.

PREFACE

I have only had a few times in my life that I knew beyond a shadow of a doubt that God had spoken to me. I am not referring to the times when He speaks through His word. I have heard His voice many times as I have either studied the scriptures or sat under the preaching and teaching of the same. I am thinking of those few remarkable moments when He makes His presence vividly real and though His voice is like a still small whisper it is unmistakably loud enough to recognize as His own.

This book was written out of one of those moments. It was in the midst of a message that I was preaching on the subject of God's leading that I knew that message would become the basis for my next book. I wanted as many people as possible to know that it was possible to know that the path they were presently walking was indeed a path ordained and directed by God.

I have included a mileposts section at the end of each chapter to help you evaluate your present walk and make the adjustments necessary to take your next step only as God is Leading.

Scripture taken from the New King James Version®. Copyright © 1982 by Thomas Nelson, Inc. Used by permission. All rights reserved

Chapter One

TIME TO LEAVE EGYPT

Our journey always begins in Egypt. At least our spiritual journeys do. Egypt early on in biblical typology symbolizes the world.

It is a place of captivity. As with Israel at the time of the Exodus, everyone alive at that moment had been born into slavery. They knew nothing else.

Surely there were stories of a place called the Promised Land, but for the most part they were just that: stories. Four hundred years had brought forth a people that assumed their destiny was simply to make bricks and build fabulous structures to the glory of the Pharaoh.

But God heard the cry of the few. He honored his

promises to deliver His people from captivity and His plan was to do so with a mighty hand.

Enter Moses. Though he began forty years earlier with a less than spectacular deliverance of the people, he returned. He had spent the previous four decades on the back side of the desert. God had been preparing this former prince of Egypt to be the one who would lead His people out of the shadows of slavery into the sunshine of salvation. It was time to leave Egypt.

This journey would begin with all of the excitement and expectation that accompanies most adventures. With a powerful hand God would demonstrate to the greatest power on Earth, that He could set His people free.

All of this was to transpire on time as God's purpose was revealed. Never late, but also never early, God would show forth His will for His people. Their response was to follow His leading.

As with all of us, discovering God's will is only the beginning. Following His lead until His will is fully accomplished is the more difficult part of all this.

It is easy to fill a room with conferees if the breakout session is titled, "How To Know the Will of God." Dozens will line up to find God's will—especially if God's will lines up perfectly with their plans.

You can narrow the crowd a bit if you add two words to the conference title: "How To Know AND DO the Will of God." Plenty of people want to know, few want to do.

If you want to get down to the true disciples or at least filter out some of the less committed, you need only to completely rename your conference. Try this: "How To Follow God Unconditionally."

Now we have gotten down to the core group of sold out for Jesus disciples. But you could even tighten the focus more if you made the session one of self-examination. You could ask the following question. How can you know that you are being led by God?

Suddenly, your outlook becomes an in-look. You have to evaluate your present journey. You have to question whether you are really being led by God to do what you are doing. Then you have to determine whether you have spiritualized your present activity.

In other words, you may be on a good journey. It may even be a pleasant one. Perhaps you can even attribute some of your activities to godly motives. You might have even endorsed your path with a few Bible verses to back up your reasoning. But in the end, you are not being led by God.

As we take a deep look into Israel's exodus out of Egypt, I hope that you will be able to discover some checkpoints that you can use along the way. Mile markers and sign posts that will help you stay on track and be reassured that you are truly following God's leading.

Each chapter will begin with this simple statement:

Those being led by God _____.

I hope the content of each chapter helps you fill in the blank. So, let's get on the journey out of Egypt as we are led by God.

Mileposts

What part did Moses play in Israel's deliverance from Egypt?

_____
_____
_____
_____

What one truth did you learn about God's timing?

_____
_____
_____
_____

Which is more important: Your outlook or your in-look? Why?

_____
_____
_____
_____

Why is it important to know that you are being led by God?

_____
_____
_____
_____

NOTES

Chapter Two

DELIVERANCE

Those being led by God <u>have been delivered by God Himself</u>.

Our journey begins in Exodus 13:16. Much has happened in the days leading up to this verse. Some of it we will discuss as we talk about God delivering Israel from Egypt.

This verse clearly tells us that God used all of His strength to deliver Israel from Egyptian bondage: "... for by strength of hand the Lord brought us out of Egypt."

God poured all of His might into the deliverance of Israel. This demonstration of power was revealed by the plagues and miracles that had finally brought the king of Egypt to his knees and ultimately led him to send the Israelites on their way out of bondage and ultimately to the Promised Land.

The word "strength" used in this verse holds the idea of seizing. God used His mighty power to not only seize control of the Egyptians, but He also demonstrated that He was holding tightly to the Israelites throughout the entire deliverance.

Their deliverance was clearly spiritual in nature as well as physical. All of the plagues that struck Egypt were direct challenges to the gods of the Egyptians.

God was worshipped in solitude. The commandments written by the finger of God on stone tablets had clearly pronounced that there were no other gods. Egypt was overflowing with idolatry when Moses appeared on the scene to declare that Pharaoh should let the people go. One of these false gods after another were publicly disgraced as the God of Israel put His strength on display.

One by one the plagues laid waste the gods of Egypt. Pharaoh was still filled with contempt for the God of Israel when the tenth plague was unleashed. This plague demonstrated God's power over life and death. It culminated in the death of each firstborn son in every household in the land. Only those who had followed God's command to place blood on the doorposts of their homes were delivered.

Imagine the horrible cry that went up at that midnight hour, as the death angel made his way across the land of the Nile. One home after another discovered the breathless body of their firstborn son. Family upon family came to understand what it meant to be seized by the mighty hand of God.

Finally, the angel of death passed over the palace of Pharaoh. The guards could not stop his advance. The gods of Egypt were powerless at his entry. The grip of Pharaoh upon all that he thought was his was released as he held the lifeless body of his own son close to his chest. Crying out to gods that could not hear, cursing the guards who could not protect, he yielded to the powerful strength of God's mighty hand and relented. The children of Israel were sent away at his command, but in truth they had been delivered by God's own strength.

One must wonder what might have been the response of the families dwelling in the land of Goshen. Here, the children of Israel had dwelt for over 400 years awaiting this night of deliverance. They had watched as God slowly tightened His grip upon the king of Egypt. They had listened, a mere ten days prior to this night, as Moses delivered the instructions for the Passover from God.

"Then Moses called for all the elders of Israel and said to them, 'Pick out and take lambs for yourselves according to your families, and kill the Passover lamb. And you shall take a bunch of hyssop, dip it in the blood that is in the basin, and strike the lintel and the two doorposts with the blood that is in the basin. And none of you shall go out of the door of his house until morning. For the Lord will pass through to strike the Egyptians; and when He sees the blood on the lintel and on the two doorposts, the Lord will pass over the door and not allow the destroyer to come into your houses to strike you.'" ~ Exodus 12:21-23

Scripture does not tell us exactly how everyone responded to this set of instructions. All of the other plagues had affected Egypt, but the land of Goshen had been spared. This last plague required the children of Israel to prepare for the passing of the death angel over their homes as well. They would be spared only if they were to follow God's leading.

Since Scripture does not tell us how people may have responded, I have considered a few possibilities based on how I see people respond today to the shedding of blood by Jesus upon the cross.

Assuming that there is nothing new under the sun and that people are for the most part people wherever you go in this world, I have grouped the Israelites into four distinct groups.

The first group could have responded as so many do today with a total rejection of the killing of an innocent lamb. Their assumption might have been that they were sincere. They had done no great harm to anyone; kept the law; paid their taxes; loved their wives and children. You have heard the routine before.

These folks just could not see that they needed any protection from the passing over of the death angel. Even though they dwelt in the land of Goshen among thousands of fellow Israelites, the horror of this night would have been severe.

Like the wails that had wafted over the horizon from each Egyptian home affected by death's power, they too would have felt the sting of death in their home. Without the shed blood and its application to the doorposts and lintel of the home, this tenth plague would be unleashed in all of its fury.

To reject the death of Jesus as our sacrifice is no different than this scenario. Scripture is plain as it declares that Jesus came once for all to die for all mankind.

Calvin Miller writing for *Discipleship Journal* stated in his article, "The Day Death Died", "One death in all history stands above all others. It is the 'death of deaths' not because it was the most painful, but because it was also the 'death of death.'"

He went on to say in this same article, "The Bible has always spoken of sin as the cause of death. In Ezekiel 18:4 the Scripture says, 'The soul who sins is the one who will die.' The Bible indicates in the book of Genesis that man, who was created to have eternal life, lost this life through disobedience. Therefore, from Adam to Jesus, sin continued to produce death, but the atonement of Jesus Christ was the answer to the problems of man's hopelessness. Jesus' voluntary giving of Himself was the death to end all death. Through God's great heart of love, Jesus showed us that His death was in some way representative. Jesus died for all men."

The second group is similar to the first. They also have an antipathy towards the shedding of blood. There is a sense of wariness in this group, however. A desire to protect their family just in case all of this Passover business is true prompts them to procure a lamb. After all, what's the harm in having an extra lamb about the house?

I can imagine them tying the lamb securely at the door of their home on the night of the Passover. All along their street lambs are heard bleating as their blood is spilled. Each of those lambs cries out for a moment and then is silenced, but not their lamb. This lamb struggles to free itself from its leash. As the midnight hour nears it is still bleating loudly into the bloodied streets of Goshen.

Then, out of nowhere, the death angel approaches this home. The lamb senses the angel's presence and pulls violently at the piece of leather strap that ties it securely to the home. The angel pauses for a moment, but seeing no blood enters the home, and the firstborn dies.

How many today have this same identity with Jesus? They have all of the religious trappings in place. A Jesus sticker adorns the bumper of their automobile. The radio is set to a Christian station. Church attendance is quasi-regular.

Anyone on the outside would quickly see Jesus tied securely at their door. But a look on the inside would see that death's power is still ruling the hour—a father mourns the death of a son.

My third grouping would include those who are most prominently found replicated in our church pews today. These individuals would declare that they fully believe Scripture to be the inspired, infallible, and inerrant Word of God.

I join them fully in this belief. Though many in this camp would proclaim their willingness to die for the truth of scripture, they simply do not live it out in their everyday lives. Theologically, they are sound; practically they are deficient.

Several years ago I developed a certain form of anemia. It is called pernicious anemia and it presents itself like this. The body can no longer properly process vitamin B-12 which is found in meats, eggs, and milks. Vitamin B-12 must be carried through the digestive tract by a protein known as the intrinsic factor.

This allows the B-12 to be absorbed into the bloodstream and thereby the nutritional value of this vitamin is made available to the human system. In the case of pernicious anemia the body stops producing this protein. Although the meats, eggs, and milk are eaten, the benefit of vitamin B-12 is lost as it is destroyed in the digestion of the food.

This analogy fits well this third group of people who had received God's word relative to the night of the Passover. Their belief was anemic. They believed, but they did not act like they believed. They had taken in the truth, but the faith factor was missing and they simply could not benefit from the joy that should have been available on this night of deliverance.

They would have taken a lamb as Moses had directed. They would have kept it and nurtured it for the required time. The father of this household would have spilled the blood of this innocent lamb at the threshold of the door. He would have dipped the hyssop branch into the blood and applied it to the lintel and the doorposts. His family would have gathered in the house and waited for the passing of the angel of death. They would have prepared the lamb and consumed it as prescribed.

Up to this point they would have been commended. This family had done all that was required, but having done all they sat in their home and trembled. Fear gripped their hearts. Both parents would minute by minute check the health of their first born son. Though they had believed the word of God and done all to protect their family from this final plague, they dwelt in unbelief and faithlessness.

As the midnight hour approached, the family would have cringed at the screeching cries of those not under the protection of the blood. With each horrible scream, they would have huddled together and especially held their son tightly. Even in their belief, they were unable to act out what they knew to be true. Like so many Christians today, it is not a matter of not believing the Bible to be true; it is not being able to act like it is and live out a biblically based life.

The angel approaches this home and sees the blood applied as required. His mission of death is fulfilled upon each family unprotected by the blood. His determination for passing over the blood splattered home has nothing to do with the fear of those huddled inside. He sees the blood and passes over this home. Inside a father holds his son, kisses his cheek and looks deeply into his eyes—a son lives.

And now, my final grouping. Hopefully, you find yourself in this group. If not, then use this as an opportunity to make the adjustments necessary to begin living your life in joyful deliverance from Egypt's bondage.

This group may have been smaller in number than most of us would like to admit. These families followed God's word to the tee as it had been delivered by Moses. They were done with life in Egypt and willing to do whatever it took to live a victorious life on the other side of the Red Sea. They were ready to experience all that the Promised Land held for them.

As in the previous group, they would have procured a lamb and faithfully sacrificed it at the door of their home. The children would have watched as the little lamb died there. Its blood forming a pool at the threshold of the door.

They would have followed the hand of their father as he placed some of the blood on the lintel and doorposts. As his hand moved through the air placing the blood of innocence upon the doorway, they would have seen father leaving blood in the shape of a cross.

Blood now marked on the door the very places that Jesus would have bled on the cross of Calvary. The lintel marking the place where the thorns adorned his brow. The doorposts bearing the blood that would have run down from his nail-pierced hands. The threshold pooling the blood that would have coursed down His body and joined that which flowed from his nailed feet.

This family would have watched as the body of this lamb was prepared and their mother began to cook it. They would have gathered fully dressed and shoes on their feet. This was to be an unforgettable night. Soon, the angel of death would visit their street. He would stop at their door, but he would not enter to take away any lives in that home.

Together, they would have sat in the dim light and rejoiced that a lamb had given its life to protect them. With joy they would sing together and rejoice that this was their last night in captivity. And what song do you think they might sing? Though it was not written for 3400 years, I would like to imagine they sang a song like, *Victory in Jesus*. Its words are so appropriate:

> I heard an old, old story,
> How a Savior came from glory,
> How He gave His life on Calvary
> To save a wretch like me;
> I heard about His groaning,
> Of His precious blood's atoning.
> Then I repented of my sins,
> And won the victory.
>
> O victory in Jesus,
> My Savior, forever.
> He sought me and bought me
> With His redeeming blood;
> He loved me ere I knew Him,
> And all my love is due Him,
> He plunged me to victory,
> Beneath the cleansing flood.

15

Certainly, we cannot be sure how things happened exactly that night long ago in Egypt, but understanding human nature and our response to the word of God, I hold some confidence that similar responses would have been noted on that night of deliverance.

One thing is for sure: God's deliverance of Israel was permanent, as is ours. I can only find one time that the Red Sea was divided and it was to let God's people leave Egypt.

If you have been delivered, it was for good. No one has to tell you if you have experienced a Red Sea crossing. Its fact resonates in your heart. You know it to be true. Now begin to live that truth out in your everyday life.

The very first evidence that you are being led by God is the fact of your deliverance. Without this, you cannot even begin this journey. Deliverance can be yours today for the asking. Simply repent from your sins and believe that the sacrifice of Jesus is enough to deliver you.

Like the blood of a lamb on the doorposts of the Israelites, the blood shed on the cross can keep you safe at the passing of death's angel. If you are a believer having trusted Christ as your personal Lord and Savior, then now is the time to claim your victory in Jesus and walk out of Egypt as God leads.

If you have never accepted Christ and had the blood of the cross applied to the door of your heart, you are still captive in a spiritual Egypt and in need of a rescue. The death angel is surely on his way since all of us will one day face our final moment in this life.

Why not call upon Jesus now? You do not need a lamb to sacrifice, because The Lamb of God has already been sacrificed for you. Trust His shed blood as it is applied to your life. He will immediately give you eternal life and you can rest assured that you will be saved when death knocks on your door.

Mileposts

Why did the children of Israel need to be delivered from Egypt?

_____

_____

_____

_____

What significance does the Passover hold for believers?

_____

_____

_____

_____

What four scenarios does the author give as responses to the Passover?

_____

_____

_____

_____

Why was it required that the lamb's blood be spilled?

_____

_____

_____

_____

How many households were affected by the passing of the angel of death?

_____

_____

_____

_____

What familiar symbol was formed by the application of the blood on the door of each Israelite home?

_____

_____

_____

_____

NOTES

Chapter Three

FOLLOWING WITHOUT QUESTION

Those being led by God <u>follow without question</u>.

Deliverance is the easy part of being led by God.

And your response to that statement is most likely a resounding gasp as you try to catch your breath. Deliverance is really easy though. When you consider the fact that you are in bondage and that the greatest army in the world is keeping you there, deliverance is really easy.

It is easy, because it all depends upon God's power being released to set you free. All you must do is prepare to leave. Just as the children of Israel did on that Passover night.

All of the details of their deliverance were choreographed by God. He chose all of the plagues and directed their administration upon the Egyptians. Those who prepared a lamb and applied the blood to their doorways went out the next morning on a glorious journey that would take them directly to the Promised Land.

Wrong!

Sometimes God's way will not be the quickest way. At times we will find ourselves developing a questioning attitude. You know the routine. If you have not asked the question, you have been asked the question. It usually comes from the backseat of your auto and it usually comes early and often.

"Are we there yet?"

Now we expect children to ask such questions. They cannot properly access time and distance. It is easy for them to grow disgruntled quickly and start questioning your ability to get them to the appointed destination in the timeframe that they are expecting.

But we are not children or at least we should not be acting like children. This is the very reason that I stated that deliverance was the easiest part of being led by God. The real walk of faith begins immediately after the shackles of bondage fall away.

The trip from Egypt to the Promised Land would normally take about two weeks. It could have been slowed a bit when you consider that one million people or more could have been making this journey. At any rate, it was a lot shorter journey than that which Israel took.

Interestingly, God did not take them from the very outset on the direct route. He began by leading Israel on a particular way that lead them into a trap. At least that is the way it looked to Pharaoh who early the next morning had changed his mind about letting his slave laborers leave Egypt.

"Then it came to pass, when Pharaoh had let the people go, that God did not lead them by way of the land of the Philistines, although that was near; for God said, 'Lest perhaps the people change their minds when they see war, and return to Egypt.' So God led the people around by way of the wilderness of the Red Sea. And the children of Israel went up in orderly ranks out of the land of Egypt."~Exodus 13:17-18

There are very few times, if any, that we will be able to know why God is leading us along a certain path. We are almost certain to ask, "Are we there yet?"

The present generation does not know of a world without the microwave or the myriad of other quick and easy apparatuses that have caused us to adopt an attitude of instant gratification.

We want it now and fast. Shortcuts abound in the computer world and we have grown accustomed to taking them regularly. The only problem is that all of this quick fix and rapid remedy has carried over into other areas of our lives.

We want our fast food really fast. Don't you dare make me wait more than a few minutes in line at McDonald's. Cars are always inching forward at the stop light and you must be very careful when your light turns green for inevitably two or three more cars will run their light while it is glaring red.

What we miss in all of this is the fact that God is protecting us by His divine delay. God purposefully led them the long way and into what seemed like a trap at the edge of the Red Sea, because He knew their hearts.

These people had never seen war. They had all been born into slavery. They made no decisions on their own. They worked when and where they were told. They built what the taskmaster said to build. Their advice was never asked for nor rendered.

Before we come to Christ, it may appear that we have all of the freedom to make our own decisions, but honestly, just the opposite is true. We are slaves to sin. We do what sin commands and we have no choice in the matter.

It is when deliverance comes that we begin to make real choices. We have all of the potential to make terrible choices, but thank God, He is leading us. Though it might seem like the long way around, He is really protecting us from changing our minds and scurrying back into captivity. Remember, that this was a real tendency in the children of Israel. Every time they faced difficulty someone would come up with the idea of going back to Egypt.

God's leading will always be a way of faith. Faith will always be without sight for if we could see, then it would not be faith at all. The way that God leads is a proving ground for our faith. Moses wrote of their wilderness journey as he recorded the history of Israel.

"And you shall remember that the Lord your God led you all the way these forty years in the wilderness, to humble you and test you, to know what was in your heart, whether you would keep His commandments or not.~Deuteronomy 8:2

We will never be in peril when we travel in the place that God had led us. Times may be trying. They may be tough, but God's purpose is not to harm us. He wants us to know what is really in our hearts and to rid us of our tendency to flee back to Egypt.

How can this be possible in our Christian walk? Why can we follow Him even when the way seems long? What will change our hearts and keep us from asking, "Are we there yet?"

Everything changes the moment we recognize Him as The Good Shepherd. The shepherd is always there to protect the sheep. The shepherd will lay down his life for the sheep, just as Christ laid down His life for us.

It always comes back to the blood. It was the blood on the doorposts of the homes that protected them on the night of the Passover. It is the blood on the cross that proves that Christ lays down His life for the sheep.

God led Israel by another way to keep them from facing the enemy too soon. They would face enemies along the way, but those times would come later after they learned to trust God. They would come to know His voice as the Good Shepherd and follow Him wherever He led.

It may have been to green pastures or beside still waters as Psalm 23 tells us. But this Psalm also declares that the Shepherd prepares a table in the presence of the enemy. The good news is that His rod and staff are always ready to protect from the attack of the enemy.

The way may seem far, but we can follow because we know where we are headed. The believer knows that heaven is the final destination. We travel on the King's highway. This road was paved by God Himself in the shed blood of His own Son. Only the redeemed can travel there and the way has been rendered safe from all attacks of the enemy. So said Isaiah:

"A highway shall be there, and a road, and it shall be called the Highway of Holiness. The unclean shall not pass over it, but it shall be for others. Whoever walks the road, although a fool, shall not go astray. No lion shall be there, nor shall any ravenous beast go up on it; it shall not be found there. But the redeemed shall walk there, and the ransomed of the Lord shall return, and come to Zion with singing, with everlasting joy on their heads. They shall obtain joy and gladness, and sorrow and sighing shall flee away."~Isaiah 35:8-10

Delivered and moving out of Egypt without question. Now you know two of the seven ways to be sure that God is leading you.

"Are we there yet?" That's a good question. So, let's move on to the next chapter and the next milepost that encourages you to know you are being led by God.

Mileposts

Are there times in your life where God's ways seem mysterious? How?

_____
_____
_____
_____

Why did God lead the children of Israel on a longer journey to the promised land than was necessary?

_____
_____
_____
_____

What part does faith play when things in your life do not go as expected?

_____
_____
_____
_____

How do our questions bring added confusion to the process of knowing whether God is leading us or not?

_____
_____
_____
_____

Recount one incident in your life where you asked, "Are we there yet?

_____

_____

_____

_____

How comforting is it as a believer to know that God fills the role of being our Good Shepherd?

_____

_____

_____

_____

NOTES

Chapter Four

FOLLOWING IN AN ORDERLY MANNER

Those being led by God <u>should follow in an orderly manner</u>.

And the children of Israel went up in orderly ranks out of the land of Egypt."~Exodus 13:18b

If deliverance is the easiest part of knowing you are being led by God, then following in an orderly manner has to be the most difficult. Every part of our being resists order. We live in a chaotic world that is filled with disorder. Everything is affected by the resulting disorder that sin causes.

Imagine the massive task that lay before Moses. Yesterday all of Israel lived in Goshen and labored in the slave camps of the Pharaoh. Miserable conditions to say the least, but at least there was order. Everyone knew exactly what the parameters were. The taskmasters made it plain through the tip of the whip.

But today...today would be different. Today over one million former slaves would move out of Goshen and begin the journey towards the Promised Land.

It is amazing to me that Scripture records the little sentence at the end of verse 18. What could be seen as a side note in truth is one of the main markers that help us determine whether we are being led by God or not in whatever journey we happen to be taking at the moment.

God is a God of order. From the very beginning of time and the recording of Scripture, we see God bringing order to the chaos of this world. In Genesis, God appears without explanation to bring order and light to our world.

"In the beginning God created the heavens and the earth. The earth was without form, and void; and darkness was on the face of the deep. And the Spirit of God was hovering over the face of the waters. Then God said, 'Let there be light'; and there was light."~Genesis 1:1-3

Scripture goes on to inform us that God is not the author of confusion as we read in 1 Corinthians 14:33, "For God is not the author of confusion but of peace, as in all the churches of the saints." Clearly, if there is disorder and confusion, we have left God out somewhere along the way.

We can then conclude that orderliness is a direct indication that we are being led by God. But orderliness is not always easy to accomplish. You probably have noticed that life can be very messy. It becomes even more messy when we are not being led by God on our journey.

It would be easier if we journeyed alone.

Well, that's a grand thought, but the reality of a solo journey through life is just not available to us. God made it very clear from the beginning that it was not good for man to be alone.

Upon every act of creation, God declared that it was good and even very good. The first time the phrase "not good" was used is when it refers to the aloneness of man. God openly stated, "And the Lord God said, 'It is not good that man should be alone; I will make him a helper comparable to him.'"~Genesis 2:18

It may not have been good for Adam to be alone, but at least there was order. How long everything would have remained as such, we do not know. This much is evident. Soon after Eve was formed and presented to Adam, disorder through sin entered into the world. Anytime two or more of us get together there will be some form of disorder.

The only possibility of reestablishing order is when we make sure that we are following God. The way of order was set forth by God. All Adam and Eve had to do was follow God. They simply had to make sure that God was leading and the results would have been order. They chose to sin and in doing so refused to follow God's lead. The result was disorder that all of us still feel the reverberations from to this day.

If we agree to the fact that we will never live our lives totally alone, then we must settle very quickly this matter of orderly living. Orderliness is a primary indicator of being led by God.

The word translated "orderly" comes from the Hebrew word, "châmûsh". It is pronounced khaw-moosh. It is a term used mostly in a military sense. It speaks of the rank order of soldiers as they march as one unit. The idea is that of being harnessed in all of your gear as an able-bodied, staunch soldier.

A good soldier understands the value of unity. A fighting force of soldiers operates as if they are yoked together. It's the old adage, "all for one and one for all". There is the pledge of no soldier left behind. Valor is not of independent grasp; it is earned by the unit.

Our unity of fellowship at any level can be directly attributed to our unity with God. We are yoked with Him for this journey, but it is important to keep ourselves in the right perspective as we progress along life's way under God's direction.

Not only are we not able to make this journey alone, we are more than likely to make it in a group. It may not be one million plus like the Israelites leaving Egypt, but we will probably find ourselves in some collection of people. It may be a church group, school class, or a team of workers on a job site. We will inevitably have to interact like a battalion of soldiers at some point. Our survival and success will be directly connected to us being unified under the leading of God.

God desires to lead us in every relationship we encounter along life's journey. If order is not evident in your daily interactions with others, you can be sure that God is not leading you at this time.

Imagine our connection to God's leadership this way. Take the two numbers: zero and one. You and I are the zero. God is the one. There are two possible ways to align these numbers, but with vast differences in the results.

If I try to lead my life the result of that will be an alignment that looks like this:

01

There you have the very number that God declared was not good back in the Garden of Eden. Remember, the old song, "One"? It opens with the line, "One is the loneliest number that you'll ever do." When we put ourselves in the lead ahead of God, the results are just loneliness.

However, if I realign my life and let God lead me then the results would look like this:

10

What a difference from this little realignment! The number one is transformed into a ten. The number ten has come to mean the very best. When we rate someone or something and they are at the top we give them a ten. If you want a life of order, put God into the lead and you just follow. The result easily ranks as a ten.

But it gets better! God provided for Adam a woman to walk alongside him through life. Eve, formed from Adam's side, was to be his helpmate. She would be a lifelong companion as they walked through life together. What do you think would happen if two zeroes like Adam and Eve were to get together and realign their lives behind the leadership of God?

If indeed God is leading a couple and we maintain our analogy of zeroes and ones the results would look like this:

100

Are you beginning to get the picture? Each time we harness ourselves together under the leadership of God our effectiveness increases.

Add a child to a family as another zero and you have:

1000

Let this family join a church of one hundred fellow believers, all of them zeros as well, and you now have:

100,000

If only two of these congregations come together in unity of faith and decide that together they will be under the divine leadership of God, the resulting number would be:

10,000,000

And there you have it! With only one couple, one child, and one congregation of believers joining with one other under the leadership of God, you have the effective force of an army ten times more in number than all the children of Israel that left out of Egypt on a journey to the Promised Land.

You can only move such a mighty force when it is done so in order. As it was with Israel, so it must be in our lives. We must move under God's leadership with rank order. Let God lead and all we must do is keep all of the zeroes in their proper places.

From this point on in your journey, you can always make unity and order be a checkpoint in determining God's leading in your life. Remember that you must take evaluations at every level of your life to determine if God truly is leading you on your journey.

If there is disunity in your thought life and disorder in your planning, stop now and place God back in front. Let Him have control of you private life. Let Him guide you through every decision and you will be amazed at the peace that will come. It will be a peace that passes all understanding (Philippians 4:7)

In your marriage, make sure that every hint of disunity and disorder is resolved quickly. As I said earlier in this chapter, Adam was living a life of order until Eve came along, but God declared that his life of aloneness was not good.

Make the concept of marching together through life a priority. Let no man or woman be left behind as you fight the good fight together. Communicate regularly the goal of your life.

Notice I did not say goals. There may be some subsets of goals that you have as a couple, but your ultimate goal is heaven, the Promised Land. God has set you free to travel together across the Red Sea, through the wilderness, and arrive safely on the other side. Talk together about heaven and avoid the tendency when things get tough to resort to aloneness back in Egypt.

As part of a congregation...you are part of a congregation aren't you? Remember God has plainly commanded, "... not forsaking the assembling of ourselves together, as is the manner of some, but exhorting one another, and so much the more as you see the Day approaching."~Hebrews 10:25

As part of a congregation, you must serve together in harmony. Be like good soldiers harnessed for battle and linked together in rank order. Determine your place in God's army and serve well there. Do not strive to attain the rank of another. Valor belongs to the unit not to the individual. Walk in unity. Paul made this a priority in his letters to the early church:

"I, therefore, the prisoner of the Lord, beseech you to walk worthy of the calling with which you were called, with all lowliness and gentleness, with longsuffering, bearing with one another in love, endeavoring to keep the unity of the Spirit in the bond of peace. There is one body and one Spirit, just as you were called in one hope of your calling; one Lord, one faith, one baptism; one God and Father of all, who is above all, and through all, and in you all."~Ephesians 4:1-6

There it is again! The number one in its proper place. You just keep Number One where He should be and all of the zeroes of life will fall into their correct position. After all, it doesn't matter which zero comes first, but it will always matter that God comes first as He leads you on in your journey.

Mileposts

How important is it to the Christian life to live a life of order?

_____

_____

_____

_____

Why was an orderly departure from Egypt so important to the Israelites?

_____

_____

_____

_____

What is the number one rule for there to be proper order in your life?

_____

_____

_____

_____

When did Israel actually begin to prepare for their departure from Egypt?

_____

_____

_____

_____

What areas of your life are presently in disorder?

_____

_____

_____

_____

What steps are you ready to take to bring order to your life?

_____

_____

_____

_____

NOTES

Chapter Five

WALKING IN THE LIGHT

Those being led by God <u>will walk in the light</u>.

Many years ago our home was graced with a visitor from Kenya. His name was Elijah Buconyori. Elijah was not his given name. He had changed his birth name to reflect his rebirth into the Kingdom of God.

Elijah told a story about walking to his home in the dark. He explained that he would always tie the lantern he carried onto the end of a long pole. He would then extend the pole out in front of him as he walked along jungle paths back to his village.

The light, he told us, was a comfort to him. It pierced the darkness and no matter how dark the night was his light could not be extinguished by it. Each step he took pushed the light further into the darkness. Each step caused whatever creatures there were lurking in the dark to run for cover. Their movement gave them away, but he was encouraged by the sound they were making. He knew that his lantern on a pole was clearing the path of all things that might cause him harm.

God did something very similar for the children of Israel as they began their exodus from Egypt. He extended the light of His own presence into this darkened world. He became their lantern on a pole to go before them into the darkness.

"And the Lord went before them by day in a pillar of cloud to lead the way, and by night in a pillar of fire to give them light, so as to go by day and night. He did not take away the pillar of cloud by day or the pillar of fire by night from before the people."~Exodus 13:21-22

We clearly see God's intent to lead. He went before them—not beside them, nor behind them. He was out front throughout this entire process.

God's position and expressed desire to lead us does not preclude the fact that we all have the potential to either run ahead of God or dawdle in the shadows far removed from the pillar of fire.

Amazingly, God will allow us to do either. I have outrun God's light before and I have stories to tell that would make your hair stand on end. I have also become disenfranchised with the whole journey to the Promised Land. I start asking, "Are we there yet?" The next thing you know I've slipped off from His leading.

God knows that the dark is a natural force that tends to drive us back to His leading. He is willing to allow us to run on ahead or fall behind so we can learn again and again that the safest place of all is in the light.

The cloud by day and the pillar of fire by night became the conductor for this train of refugees flooding back to their homeland. The instructions were clear. Move only when the cloud or the pillar moved. It was a visible platform from which God revealed His will to the people.

You may be asking at this point, why don't we have such an instrument to guide us? You may be thinking that you could use a heavenly GPS to guide you through the traffic of life. Could our journey be simpler if God just showed up visibly and walked before us?

I suppose it might be, but you will find that the children of Israel still made some horrible decisions even with a cloud and a pillar in their presence. I do the same thing when I am using the GPS in my vehicle. I hear the instructions, but I refuse to follow them. I assume that I know better and off I go with the lady inside my GPS repeating over and over, "Recalculating, recalculating."

God is better than a GPS. He never recalculates. He will not allow us to simply design our own path and then ask Him to come along for the ride. His will for us is inviolable. He has declared that He alone is God and that He changes not. (Malachi 3:6)

Israel knew when to move or when to stay according to the movement of the cloud. "Whenever the cloud was taken up from above the tabernacle, the children of Israel would go onward in all their journeys. But if the cloud was not taken up, then they did not journey till the day that it was taken up. For the cloud of the Lord *was* above the tabernacle by day, and fire was over it by night, in the sight of all the house of Israel, throughout all their journeys."~Exodus 40:36-38

We may not have a cloud or a pillar, but we have something, or should I say Someone, that is much better. The Holy Spirit of God has taken up residence in each believer. We have His constant counsel to guide us in every decision that we make. He is better than a light extended on a pole into the darkness. That light might go out, but He is the very essence of God. Since God has declared Himself to be light (1 John 1:5) and the Holy Spirit is God, then we can be assured that we will always walk in the light.

Paul Lee Tan in his book, *Encyclopedia of 7700 Illustrations: Signs of the Times*, recounts the following war story:

During the second World War an aircraft carrier was out in the North Atlantic. As it was engaged in war, its six pilots took off the carrier to scout out some enemy submarines. While these pilots were gone, the captain of the ship issued an alarm. The button was pushed, and every light on that ship was extinguished.

Eventually these pilots started to come back toward the mother ship, and realizing that she was down there somewhere, although they couldn't find her, they radioed the ship: "Give us light, we're coming home."

The radio operator on the ship radioed back: "Order—blackout. I can't give you light."

Another pilot picked up his radio and said, "Just give us some light, and we'll make it."

And the radio operator said, "No light—blackout."

The third pilot picked up his radio, and he said, "Give us just one light, and we'll land."

The operator could do no more. He reached over, turned the switch, and broke radio contact. Six red-blooded aviators, in the prime of manhood, went down in the cold, north Atlantic Ocean and out into eternity.

You and I never have to worry about a time when we will hear a reply from heaven, "No light—blackout." We can rejoice in that fact. I did not say that it might not get dark. I did not say that the sun may be blotted out for a time. My guarantee is that no matter how dark the circumstances are there will always be the light of heaven available like a light extended on a pole.

Several verses of Scripture come to mind when I think about this milepost along the journey towards the Promised Land. As we validate our steps and make sure that God is leading us here are some assurances that we can hide in our hearts. Each one can be like an automatic night light that comes on when the room gets dark.

"Then Jesus spoke to them again, saying, 'I am the light of the world. He who follows Me shall not walk in darkness, but have the light of life.'"~John 8:12

"In Him was life, and the life was the light of men. And the light shines in the darkness, and the darkness did not comprehend it."~John 1:4

"The Lord is my light and my salvation; Whom shall I fear?"~Psalm 27:1

"There shall be no night there: They need no lamp nor light of the sun, for the Lord God gives them light. And they shall reign forever and ever."~Revelation 22:5

And this is my personal favorite when it comes to thinking about the importance of light as we walk while He leads us:

"Who among you fears the Lord? Who obeys the voice of His Servant? Who walks in darkness And has no light? Let him trust in the name of the Lord and rely upon his God. Look, all you who kindle a fire, who encircle yourselves with sparks: walk in the light of your fire and in the sparks you have kindled—this you shall have from My hand: you shall lie down in torment."~Isaiah 50:10-11

God does not hide the fact that there will be times when it gets very dark. It is in those times that we sometimes lose our spiritual composure. We grow fearful and in a futile attempt, we try to make our own feeble light. Don't do it!

These verses from Isaiah make it very plain that trying to create your own light will only lead to torment. Make sure that the light you are walking in is not of your own making. I affectionately call this, "Flick Your BIC theology".

I created this catch phrase from the old commercials for the BIC lighter. Their mantra was that you could always "Flick Your BIC". This may have made a cute commercial, but it will not work in our journey to the Promised Land. Flicking your BIC will only lead to disgrace.

Verse 10 above begins with three questions. The last of these asks, "Who walks in darkness and has no light?" The inference is clear that the questions are asked of believers.

The answer for the dark times is to put your trust in God alone. As we have seen already, since God is light, we can fully place our confidence in Him to provide for us a way to dispel the darkness. I call this "Spiritual Radar".

When it's too dark to see, we can rely upon God like a radar beam bouncing back in the night. We can be very sure that God will not leave us without a way to walk in the light.

My pastor used to say to me when times were tough and I couldn't see a way out of my situation, "Son, it's getting gloriously darker!" Now, that is when you turn on your spiritual radar and keep walking as He leads.

Mileposts

In what two ways did God display His daily presence in the life of the Israelites?

_____
_____
_____
_____

Describe the contrast between walking in the light and walking in darkness.

_____
_____
_____
_____

What are the consequences of trying to create your own light?

_____
_____
_____
_____

Describe a recent time in your life that seemed dark. Why was finding the light of God so important?

_____
_____
_____
_____

NOTES

Chapter Six

PURSUED BY AN ENEMY

Those being led by God <u>will be pursued by an enemy</u>.

Now isn't that great news! We get ourselves delivered by the mighty hand of God. We finally come to the place in our walk that we stop questioning God's ability to lead us. We get our lives in order and begin to walk in unity. We are rejoicing in the fact that God has promised us light for every step of the journey.

Then we look over our shoulder and see the enemy fast approaching. I thought somebody said this would be easy or at least a short little exercise in faith.

Wrong again!

Here's where we are in the exodus story. Israel has left Egypt's control, but they have not yet passed the city limits of Egypt. The direction that they have been led by God puts them along the edge of the Red Sea. They are in the tip of a funnel and around a million folks are all trying to squeeze through at one time.

The Red Sea lies before them like a great impassable wall and Pharaoh has gotten over his grief from the death of his son quickly. He has replaced his sorrow with anger and bitterness and decides to send his armies out to recapture the Israelites and bring them back under his heavy hand of captivity.

The incident is recorded in Exodus 14. "And the Lord hardened the heart of Pharaoh king of Egypt, and he pursued the children of Israel; and the children of Israel went out with boldness. So the Egyptians pursued them, all the horses and chariots of Pharaoh, his horsemen and his army, and overtook them camping by the sea beside Pi Hahiroth, before Baal Zephon."~Exodus 14:8-9

Scripture often gives us the geographical names where certain historical narratives were conducted. A look into these names and their meaning can often help us understand what was transpiring and give us indication of the value this account adds to our walk.

As Israel left Egypt God led them on a way that would prevent direct conflict with the enemies that lay before them. But it is interesting that it was God that hardened the heart of Pharaoh concerning the children of Israel.

The enemy was actually prompted by God's actions to chase Israel down and attempt a recapture. It was God who led them into a place where they could actually be captured unless He were to intercede.

That place was near unto Pi Hahiroth before you come to Baal Zephon. If you remember my GPS reference which I used earlier, I made the analogy that often we refuse to follow the advice we are receiving from the unit and we find ourselves in predicaments. Here was a predicament that was all God's idea.

The place named Pi Hahiroth can be loosely translated as "the mouth of the gorge." The other place near there was Baal Zephon and its name came from the god of the Philistines and the word for darkness and gloom.

This would be a good time for the music to start a crescendo and we would wait for something to jump out of the dark and grab us. In other words, Israel was in a real fix.

They were camping in the mouth of a deep, dark, foreboding gorge that emptied out onto the beach at the brink of the Red Sea. Pharaoh's army must have thought that they had hit the jackpot. These slaves would be back making bricks for the next pyramid in no time at all.

What they did not know was that all of this had been orchestrated by God Himself. Never underestimate God's ability to get us out of a pinch. Never let the geography of circumstance take away your joy or squash your faith!

If we are to follow God as He leads us, we will be pursued by an enemy. This is one of the great ways to know that we are being led by God. Look over your shoulder. If you do not see an enemy hot on your heels then you had better question whether you are being led by God or not.

God had led the children of Israel to this very place and then stirred up the enemy to follow. Having the enemy follow you and even surround you is a hallmark of being led by God. This one milepost cannot be denied or avoided. The enemy will surely come when you are being led by God.

A story comes to mind that is attributed to the military life of Lieutenant General Lewis Burwell "Chesty" Puller. His exact words may be disputed, but his heroic life matches the spirit of the situation he faced during the Korean War. In the Battle of Chosin Reservoir, the Chinese military surrounded the men that Puller was leading.

Chesty calmly surveyed the hopeless situation and said, "They're on our right, they're on our left, they're in front of us, they're behind us; they can't get away from us this time."

When we are surrounded by our enemies, it is time to reflect on God's leading in getting us into that situation. If He has led us there, then it is His responsibility to lead us out of the same.

Jesus faced an enemy continually in the years of His ministry here on earth. No one would question whether He was being led by God, yet He was continually hounded by the forces of hell itself.

Early in His ministry, He was led by the Spirit into the wilderness. There He was directly confronted by Satan and three times dealt with severe temptation. In each case He answered the accusations and innuendos of the devil with three words, "It is written!" (Matthew 4 and Luke 4)

Later in His ministry He said to His disciples, "Woe to you when all men speak well of you, for so did their fathers to the false prophets."~Luke 6:26

It is simply unnatural for a follower of God to not have an enemy following close on his heels. Take a look over your shoulder today. You can be blessed if you see the dust cloud rising on the horizon. You can be sure that God is leading you on your journey when you look on every side and see the enemy gathered.

Take the general's attitude when this occurs in your life. "They can't get away from us this time!"

We will never step right out of Egypt into the Promised Land. God will lead us on a journey that will prepare and strengthen us. Our faith will be tested and it will grow accordingly.

We have examined five of the seven ways we can know that God is leading us. They are:

Those who are led by God have been delivered.

Those who are led by God follow without question.

Those who are led by God follow in an orderly manner.

Those who are led by God walk in the light.

Those who are led by God will be pursued by an enemy.

Mileposts

What was Pharaoh's response to Israel's departure from Egypt?

_____
_____
_____
_____

How does God use the enemy's pursuit to increase our faith?

_____
_____
_____
_____

At what point, if ever, does an enemy give up its pursuit of a believer?

_____
_____
_____
_____

Why does God lead us in situations that seem to have no way of escape?

_____
_____
_____
_____

Taking a quick look over your shoulder, who or what is pursuing you today?

_____

_____

_____

_____

NOTES

Chapter Seven

THE SALVATION OF THE LORD

Those who are being led by God <u>shall see the salvation of the Lord</u>.

The children of Israel are trapped. The Red Sea stretches before them and the armies of Egypt are aligned behind them. Nothing short of a miracle is going to help alleviate their problem.

Ah, but it is God who has led them to this place. It is the same God who had promised to never forsake them. It is this God who said in the times of the Judges, "I led you up from Egypt and brought you to the land of which I swore to your fathers; and I said, 'I will never break My covenant with you.'"~Judges 2:1

Their God had delivered them with might and power and demonstrated His strength to protect as the death angel passed over their homes. They had left with boldness and on the way out had literally dispossessed the Egyptians of all their riches. Theirs had been a glorious display of salvation.

But now they were in a fix. They were about to be defeated before they had even crossed the border out of Egypt. What did they need?

They needed the salvation of the Lord. But wait. Had they not already experienced salvation? Isn't salvation a one-time event? Salvation is supposed to be a completed process that never must be visited again, right? Well, yes and no.

Salvation really takes place in a continuum. We are saved completely and forever in a moment of time. We are in that instant saved from the penalty of sin. Like Israel, we are delivered from bondage to freedom, from darkness to light, and from death to life.

We are being saved, however, from the power of sin on a daily basis. This part of salvation is ongoing. It happens all the time as we walk through life following God's lead. Sometimes that journey takes us to hard places and in those moments we need salvation to be made evident in a new and powerful fashion.

This is where Israel was on the shoreline of the Red Sea. Their faith was faltering. Fear had taken them captive and their doubts led them to complaining. They immediately thought that they would have been better off back in Egypt. They were ready to throw in the towel before the fight had even begun. Nothing short of salvation would do and this is exactly what God's word through Moses informed them of at that moment.

"And Moses said to the people, 'Do not be afraid. Stand still, and see the salvation of the Lord, which He will accomplish for you today.'"~Exodus 14:13a

Here they were, having just witnessed the most demonstrative act of God they had ever seen in their lives. A pillar of fire was flaming brightly before them and yet they were filled with fear. They were beginning to break into a dead heat back into captivity. The fight or flight decision had been made and they had chosen flight.

But Moses stood before them in reassurance and proclaimed, "Stand still!" This is the place we must come to at times. We must calm all of our fears and just stand still. The psalmist said it best, "Be still, and know that I am God; I will be exalted among the nations, I will be exalted in the earth! The Lord of hosts is with us; the God of Jacob is our refuge."~Psalm 46:10-11

When it looks like all is lost, be still. When the enemy had chased us down, be still. When we are seemingly trapped at the mouth of a darkened gorge, be still.

Be still and then you will know once again that He is the God that is ready to save you not only from the penalty (bondage) of your sin, but also to deliver you in those moments from the very power of sin unleashed like an Egyptian army against you. "Stand still and see the salvation of the Lord!"

Saved from the penalty of sin and the power of sin leads us to that future day when we will be saved from the very presence of sin. We will finally step into heaven where sin cannot enter and we will never again have to face the enemy on the brink of the Red Sea.

Until that day, Israel's encounter with the Egyptian army gives us some deep insights into how we are to respond when sin's power is unleashed against us by the enemy.

First, we must see our helplessness. The verse from Exodus 14:13 shown above tells us that God is going to provide a salvation that He will accomplish alone. Jonah came to this conclusion from the belly of the whale when he said, "Salvation is of the Lord."~Jonah 2:9 There are some situations that our help simply isn't needed nor is it sufficient. We must fall fully upon His grace and believe that He will do what He said He would do.

Second, we must be ready to be rid of lingering Egyptians. In this same verse, Moses said to the children of Israel, "For the Egyptians whom you see today, you shall see again no more forever."~Exodus 14:13b

Are there still some Egyptians hanging around in your life? It's time to let them go. They will continue to chase you and trap you in tight places. Their presence in your life will always bring you to living in fear. You will be tempted to run back to Egypt thinking it better to live under bondage than to be chased by the enemy. Let this be the day that you see these Egyptians again no more forever.

Third, we must become totally dependent. Moses told the Israelites, "The Lord will fight for you, and you shall hold your peace."~Exodus 14:14

We do not have to lift a finger in our own defense. The term hold your peace could be translated, "be quiet". God does not need our input into the matter. We must let him fight our fight for us. Remember, it was Job that got into trouble trying to give advice to God.

I know that this is not natural for us. Our reflexive thought is to stand up for ourselves; fight our own fight; sound the bugle and charge the enemy. Here's the truth: you do not have what it takes to win this battle. Only a complete surrender to God's leading will take care of this.

I wrote a devotion in my book, *Glasses in the Grass: Devotions for My Friends*, that fits well this idea of letting God fight for us. It is titled, "My Daddy Can Whip Your Daddy". Here it is from my February 23 devotion:

When little boys get together they often like to brag. They will compare notes on all sorts of things. Eventually the discussion wears thin when they have just about matched up even.

It's somewhere around this moment that one of the little fellows will say, "My daddy can whip your daddy!" How unfair! Bringing fathers into the affair!

As believers we can get into a few scrapes too. We will find ourselves in a battle with the devil as the tempter tries to drag us down. His attempts many times come as accusations against our Father.

His methods have not changed since the Garden of Eden. He comes along with his twisted statement that questions God's truthfulness. It is always formed in a question like this: "Has God really said _____." Then he leaves room for us to fill in the blank.

God has a few questions of his own for times like these. "'To whom then will you liken Me, or to whom shall I be equal?' says the Holy One. 'Have you not known? Have you not heard? The everlasting God, the Lord, the Creator of the ends of the earth, neither faints nor is weary. His understanding is unsearchable."'~Isaiah 40:25,28

In essence God gives us permission to say, "My daddy can whip your daddy!" Except in this case, we can say, "My daddy has ALREADY whipped you!"

It does not matter how big your enemy seems to be, God has never seen his equal. It does not matter how long the attack lasts, God does not grow weary. He will never pass out from exhaustion.

Don't waste your energy trying to figure out how God does this. He clearly declares that understanding Him is beyond our search.

Just poke your chest out and tell the devil, "My daddy's done whipped you and you're just too dumb to know it!" Whew! That felt good just writing that! Now go use it!

Fourth, we must function by faith. The Israelites were ready to run back to Egypt. They were casting blame on Moses for taking them out of Egypt to die in the wilderness. It was evident that their faith had a long way to go before reaching any degree of maturity.

God responded to their cries with these words, "And the Lord said to Moses, 'Why do you cry to Me? Tell the children of Israel to go forward.'"~Exodus 14:15

Here is one of those scriptural conundrums that will knock you for a loop if you are not careful. God had just told them to stand still and see the salvation of the Lord. Now in the same breath, He is telling them to go forward.

Are we serving a God that cannot make up His mind?

Of course not!

The answer is really very simple. We are to station ourselves in such a way upon the fact of our salvation that we can with full assurance move forward in faith.

Notice that God was leading in the opposite direction of Egypt. Faith never carries us backwards; we always move forward in faith.

This was not a time for crying. It was a time for carrying out our responsibility in this great deliverance. The battle belonged to the Lord. The enemy was His to deal with at the moment. Israel's part was to move forward toward the Red Sea.

Yes, you've already figured it out. They had to move forward BEFORE the sea had been opened. Faith operates not by sight. Faith does not need all of the facts detailed. Reality does not need to be in the past tense for us to act in faith.

God's word is simple. Quit crying and move forward. Do what God has required of you. No more and no less.

 Paul put it another way when it comes to our salvation and our response to it. He said to the church at Philippi, "Therefore, my beloved, as you have always obeyed, not as in my presence only, but now much more in my absence, work out your own salvation with fear and trembling; for it is God who works in you both to will and to do for His good pleasure."~Philippians 2:12

Fifth, and finally, rejoice in the victory. God gave Moses the key to opening the Red Sea and to the victory that was soon to follow.

"But lift up your rod, and stretch out your hand over the sea and divide it. And the children of Israel shall go on dry ground through the midst of the sea. And I indeed will harden the hearts of the Egyptians, and they shall follow them. So I will gain honor over Pharaoh and over all his army, his chariots, and his horsemen. Then the Egyptians shall know that I am the Lord, when I have gained honor for Myself over Pharaoh, his chariots, and his horsemen."~Exodus 14:16-18

God proved Himself that day not only to the Israelites, but to the Egyptians. Israel passed through the midst of the obstacle that lay before them moments before. They did so on dry ground. God doesn't do things half way. When faith is unleashed and God responds, there is no chance of getting bogged down in the mud of doubt.

Only now do we see God's plan fully revealed. He had hardened the heart of Pharaoh previously and caused him to come chasing after Israel. Now all of the Egyptians were to suffer the same fate, as God hardened their hearts once again.

The enemy that had been unleashed to chase Israel would now be destroyed by the same miracle that delivered God's people. As the chorus of the old hymn says, "Faith is the victory! Faith is the victory! Oh, glorious victory that overcomes the world!"

Mileposts

How important is it to be still in our daily walk as a believer?

_____

_____

_____

_____

List some of the reactions that you experience when faced with an obstacle such as the Red Sea.

_____

_____

_____

_____

List some of the reactions you experience when confronted with an enemy such as the Egyptians.

_____

_____

_____

_____

How is it possible to stand still and go forward at the same time?

_____

_____

_____

_____

If God is leading, then who is responsible for life's predicaments? In what ways?

_____

_____

_____

_____

Why does God lead us into challenges that are beyond our abilities to overcome?

_____

_____

_____

_____

NOTES

Chapter Eight

THE SONG OF VICTORY

Those who are being led by God <u>will sing a song of victory</u>.

Singing plays an important part in Israel's history. A look into the Bible will lead to many verses that recount the times that Israel sang. Sometimes their singing was in preparation for battle; others times their songs followed great victories.

Of course, we have the finest song book ever written in the Psalms. In this one book songs of all sorts are collected for our edification. These songs give us a peek into the lives of the songwriters. We can learn much from these songs.

No sooner had the children of Israel crossed the far shore of the Red Sea and watched the entire army of Pharaoh destroyed under the waves, than Moses led them in a glorious song of victory. The verses of this song were filled with the story of their delivery and praise for their great God who was the Deliverer.

This final checkpoint along the path to the Promised Land will always help us know whether God is leading our steps or not. Someone has said that only the redeemed can sing the songs of grace. I believe that to be true. You must have been delivered to sing songs of victorious deliverance.

Not only must deliverance be a prerequisite to singing songs of victory, but there can be no victory if we are never engaged in the battle. Remember though, we never fight alone. The battle is the Lord's and therefore the songs we sing will be about Him and not us. Our singing should be that of worship, for without God on our side, there would be no victories in which to participate.

The song of victory cannot be sung on the Egyptian side of the sea. To sing you must move forward by faith and cross through the sea. Previously, I mentioned an old hymn that might have been appropriate for a move of faith. It was the song, "Faith Is the Victory." Once that victory is fully experienced the song could easily change to "Victory In Jesus." In both cases all the glory belongs to God. The faith to cross through the sea was a gift from Him and the victory over the enemy was due to the miracle He provided.

Miracles are very much possible, but you will only find them when God is leading. When we trust God to lead us and we demonstrate that trust by following, then we find ourselves in the place where miracles can take place. Miracles are another good reason to sing.

Israel had both a victory and a miracle to prompt their singing. On the other side of both they began to sing. An examination of the song sung in Exodus 15 shows that Moses and the people sang in worship to the God who had delivered them from the mighty Egyptians.

"Then Moses and the children of Israel sang this song to the Lord, and spoke, saying: 'I will sing to the Lord, for He has triumphed gloriously'"!~Exodus 15:1a

When we are being led by God our songs will always give all glory to Him. Worship is to attribute worth to a person or object. The opening words of this song declare that it was God, not Israel, that had triumphed so gloriously.

If worship is to be directed toward the one being worshipped, it begs a question in the light of much of what we call worship today. The songs that are sung so often glorify men and their abilities. Many songs today often do not glorify the God who triumphed so gloriously at the crossing of Israel through the Red Sea.

This song of Moses left no details out in telling the account of God's triumph over the army of Pharaoh. So total was their destruction that he declared in Exodus 15:5 that they sank to the bottom like a stone. In verse 10 of this chapter, the song speaks of the army sinking like lead.

God is worshipped in this song as the only true God. The questions are asked, "Who is like You, O Lord, among the gods? Who is like You, glorious in holiness, fearful in praises, doing wonders?"~Exodus 15:11

The answer to these questions and others like them is always the God who leads. This victory song goes on to declare that it was God Himself that had led Israel from start to finish.

Imagine, if you can, the melody that accompanied these words, "You in Your mercy have led forth the people whom You have redeemed; You have guided them in Your strength to Your holy habitation."~Exodus 15:13

This one verse of the song speaks of a God who can lead a people out of captivity, guide them in strength through every trial, and take them to His own habitation. We serve a mighty God who deserves all of our worship as He leads our every step.

But there is another benefit of our testimony in song. Our singing will be overheard by the enemy that we must still face in the days after we have left Egypt.

"The people will hear and be afraid; sorrow will take hold of the inhabitants of Philistia. Then the chiefs of Edom will be dismayed; the mighty men of Moab, trembling will take hold of them; all the inhabitants of Canaan will melt away. Fear and dread will fall on them; by the greatness of Your arm they will be as still as a stone, till Your people pass over, O Lord, till the people pass over whom You have purchased."~Exodus 15:14-16

Can you hear the chorus of one million singers facing the journey ahead of them? Their voices carrying over the sands of Arabia, out over the desert, and falling upon the inhabitants of the lands they would occupy.

No wonder when they arrived years later at Jericho, Rahab said to the spies, "I know that the Lord has given you the land, that the terror of you has fallen on us, and that all the inhabitants of the land are fainthearted because of you. For we have heard how the Lord dried up the water of the Red Sea for you when you came out of Egypt…"~Joshua 2:9-10

Are you singing the victory song? If not, then you are not being led by God. This last checkpoint is the one that will show you the way to proclaim your dependence on God's leading to all who observe your journey.

You can be a witness to your fellow travelers and to those who would be enemies along the way to the Promised Land.

It's time to start singing.

Mileposts

What is the prerequisite to singing a song of victory?

_____
_____
_____
_____

How important are songs and singing in the life of a believer?

_____
_____
_____
_____

Who or what should be the focus of all worship?

_____
_____
_____
_____

Briefly describe what prompted the song of victory in Exodus 15.

_____
_____
_____
_____

Who are the people or groups that are affected by our songs of victory?

_____

_____

_____

_____

Write a paragraph or two describing your personal song of victory.

_____

_____

_____

_____

_____

_____

_____

_____

_____

_____

_____

_____

_____

_____

_____

_____

_____

_____

_____

_____

Conclusion

So, there you have the mileposts for your journey. These seven markers serve as checkpoints along the way. You can do a quick inventory any day and find out if God is really leading you.

Here they are again:

Those who are led by God <u>have been delivered</u>.

Those who are led by God <u>follow without question</u>.

Those who are led by God <u>follow in an orderly manner</u>.

Those who are led by God <u>walk in the light</u>.

Those who are led by God <u>will be pursued by an enemy</u>.

Those who are led by God <u>will see the salvation of the Lord</u>.

Those who are led by God <u>will sing a song of victory</u>.

The order in which they occur is very important. They are logical in their presentation, but they are also spiritually aligned.

You must be delivered from your sins and trespasses before anything else can take place. That's clearly the only place you can begin your walk with God and begin to follow His lead.

You will learn to trust Him as you take this journey and the questions will grow less frequent. The first to go will be, "Are we there yet?"

You will begin to notice that your life is becoming orderly. The Holy Spirit now dwells in you as a believer. This means that God is in you and where God is there can be no confusion.

You will be glad for the light when the dark times come, and they will. Even a small light is appreciated in a darkened room. God is light and He sent His Son, Jesus as the Light of the world.

You will find that the devil never gives up easily. Like Pharaoh, he will pursue you and do his best to destroy your testimony. Be sure though that you remember that it was God that hardened the heart of Pharaoh and it was God who drowned Pharaoh's army in the sea.

You will see the full salvation of the Lord. It will come day by day as God leads you. You are daily being saved from the power of sin if you have been delivered from its penalty. One glorious day you will be taken to a place where sin dwells no more and you will be delivered from its presence.

Finally, you can start singing. God has put a song of victory in your heart that no one can take away. If you don't know the words to this song, then begin today to put it in your heart and mind. Join thousands of others who have truly experienced victory in Jesus.

Victory in Jesus

I heard an old, old story,
How a Savior came from glory.
How He gave His life on Calvary,
To save a wretch like me.
I heard about His groaning,
Of His precious blood's atoning.
Then I repented of my sins,
And won the victory.

O victory in Jesus
My Savior, forever.
He sought me and bought me
With His redeeming blood.
He loved me ere I knew Him
And all my love is due Him.
He plunged me to victory
Beneath the cleansing flood.

ABOUT THE AUTHOR

R. E. CLARK currently serves as an associational missionary in Arkansas. He earned his D.Min. from the Southern Baptist Center in Jacksonville, Florida. He served as a pastor in four churches before beginning his service as the associational missionary to the 69 churches, missions, and ministry points of the Northwest Baptist Association in Bentonville, Arkansas. His writing comes from life experiences which include over 33 years in ministry.

Before his call to ministry he was a business owner. His devotional life deepened and writing career began in 2008 after the death of his wife Kay from Lou Gehrig's Disease. He has been blessed in his second marriage to Trudy. Trudy's first husband, a police officer, was killed in the line of duty. Together they have 8 children, 17 grandchildren, and one great-grandchild. They reside in Centerton, Arkansas.

You may contact the author through the following social media avenues:
Facebook: R.e. Clark
Twitter: GlassesnGrass
Blog: reclarkauthor.com

EXCERPTS FROM MY NEWEST DEVOTIONAL BOOK:

Life is NOT a Snapshot: It's A Mosaic

Available Fall 2013 in Print and eBook
from your favorite online reseller

January 1

Happy Resolution Day!

Your journey into this new year is just beginning. You will be walking a path towards developing a personal set of resolutions for the New Year.

If you are like most, your list is usually too long. Your intentions are well-founded and expectations are high. The problem is that the mountain you have constructed is just too steep to climb. After a few days of the new have evaporated, we take a gaze towards the peak and simply give up.

Another element that rises up to confront our list of resolutions is memory. We, umm, now what was I going to say... Oh yes, we forget.

In Psalm 119, David listed the first three "I wills" of his resolution:

"I will meditate on Your precepts." Psalm 119:15a
"I will contemplate Your ways." Psalms 119:15b
"I will delight in Your statutes." Psalms 119:16a

Then he added a fourth and final statement of resolution:

"I will not forget Your word." Psalms 119:16b

The word "forget" means to mislay. It is not so much intentionality, but carelessness that brings our resolutions to naught. I prefer to make this fourth statement of resolution positive instead negative: "I will remember Your word."

As in David's words found in Psalms 143:5, "I remember the days of old; I meditate on all Your works; I muse on the work of Your hands," so we must purposefully be mindful of God's words and works. The idea of remembering is to make mention of regularly.

This last "I will" of David is like the final paragraph of a formal resolution that begins with the phrase, BE IT FINALLY RESOLVED. No matter what has been said before, if there is no intent to perform, then the resolves become meaningless.

And this is where most of our resolutions fail. It is not that our intents were too grandiose. It was not that we lacked the ability to perform. It was not that we were challenged by forces seen or unseen and fell on the field of battle. We just forget!

In "The Lord of the Rings: The Return of the King", Aragon stands with the men of Middle Earth before the black gate of Sauron. With a "BE IT FINALLY RESOLVED" challenge to these warriors, he declares, "for Frodo!" Then he turns and rides toward the enemy.

He chose to remember what the whole battle was about even though he knew not the outcome. Whatever this year will bring to your path, be it good or bad, always remember God's word and ways.

BE IT FINALLY RESOLVED...

March 1

Defining the Wind

The professor asked his students to define the wind. After many valiant attempts by the students, most of them could only define the wind relative to the response of some object to the effect of the wind. The wind itself was left without a definitive description.

One student rose to her feet and approached the professor. As she drew within inches of his face she blew gently creating a warm breeze that traversed his skin. She returned to her seat without a word spoken.

The professor applauded. This young lady had defined the wind by demonstrating the feeling that this unseen phenomenon created as it passed by without any other evidence of its existence.

There is much in the world that can affect our feelings. Most of it is unseen and for the most part undefinable, yet we describe these things not by their reality, but by the feeling that they leave behind.

Feelings rush into existence in the first few pages of scripture. Though the word feel is not used, we understand from our own responses that feelings were active. No sooner had Adam and Eve sinned than they felt ashamed and guilty.

The results: They hid themselves from the presence of God. Or so they thought, because God found them even as they cowered under the feeling of remorse.

Without feeling we would have no response to the effect of sin. We would be like a paralytic who would not know the wind was passing over his skin since he could not feel its effect.

The danger is fully described as to sin's full effect when it is left unchecked. "This I say, therefore, and testify in the Lord, that you should no longer walk as the rest of the Gentiles walk, in the futility of their mind, having their understanding darkened, being alienated from the life of God, because of the ignorance that is in them, because of the blindness of their heart; who, being past feeling, have given themselves over to lewdness, to work all uncleanness with greediness."~Ephesians 4:17-19

Ask God to renew your feeling today. Ask Him to make you super sensitive to the wind of sin as it passes by you. Like a cold wind leaves one shivering in response to its bite, so may we be quick to react when we are tempted to be blown off course by sin.

May the cold harsh wind of this world be replaced with the warm gentle breeze of God's Spirit upon your life. This is my prayer for you today.

June 1

Case Dismissed!

The last few years have given us opportunity to examine the sordid details of lives gone awry. I speak, of course, in reference to the strange courtroom exhibitions that have been published for all to see.

The newspapers and television have been filled with the exploits of those who were well known and of those became well known simply because they were accused of breaking the law. Of course, they all are "innocent."

Some have been introduced to the swift hand of justice and our system of laws has prevailed to what seems to be the correct end. However, there are cases that simply allowed the guilty to escape the justice that they were due.

Amazing to me are the defense attorneys who must somehow believe that their client is innocent in the face of overwhelming evidence that proves otherwise. There is thankfully a court of higher justice in which all truth is revealed.

David found himself unjustly accused in Saul's court by a man named Cush. This man had told Saul that David could not be trusted as a friend and that David's intent was to bring harm to the king.

David's appeal was not to the judgment seat of men, but to the highest court which has as its judge the Ruler of the universe, God Himself. David proclaims, "My defense is of God, who saves the upright in heart."~Psalms 7:10

We do not hear David offering lame excuses. He is not placing blame on others. He is not creating sufficient doubt to sway a jury. He simply declares his defense to be in God.

Literally, God is his alibi. This is true because God knows his heart. There is no dishonesty before God. Excuses and pseudo-sorrow will not carry the day as we stand before God's justice.

God saves only the upright in heart. This has nothing to do with perfection or purity. This is not the sinless heart in full view of all. It is the honest heart.

Bring your case before the Lord today. Do not come with your attorney of pride nor your councilor of deceit. Come with the full acceptance of knowing that God knows all the secrets of your heart and fall forthrightly on the mercy of the court.

Only then can you hear the sweet words of grace, "Case dismissed!"

September 1

Time to Change

What is the one thing that people resist more than anything else in the world? Go ahead and take your time answering this question. I want to give you plenty of time to CHANGE your mind. While you are thinking, would you happen to have CHANGE for a dollar? Don't forget that it's only a few weeks until the season CHANGES and the leaves will all start to CHANGE colors. Whose turn is it anyway to CHANGE the baby's diaper?

Do you give up? You should know this. I've given you lots of hints. What is the one thing that people resist more than anything else in the world: CHANGE!

Someone said that the biggest room in the world is the room for change, but I think that few of us have ever spent much time in it. Jesus presented to His disciples principles that demanded radical change in their lives. They had spent years ingrained in rhetoric and religion. They had come to accept their position in life. They assumed that they were just part of the rank and file, but Jesus took them into the changing room as He drew near to the end of His earthly ministry.

Jesus called the disciples together into what is familiarly called the upper room. There they participated in the Passover meal. Then Jesus, "rose from supper and laid aside His garments, took a towel and girded Himself. After that, He poured water into a basin and began to wash the disciples' feet, and to wipe them with the towel with which He was girded. So when He had washed their feet, taken His garments, and sat down again, He said to them, "Do you know what I have done to you? You call Me Teacher and Lord, and you say well, for so I am. If I then, your Lord and Teacher, have washed your feet, you also ought to wash one another's feet. For I have given you an example, that you should do as I have done to you."~John 13:4-5, 12-15

One of the greatest changes that takes place in a believer is the transformation to servanthood. G.T. Niles said, "It is easier to dole out services than to be servants." This is so true in our day. If we are not careful with our kindness and mercy, we can become just another welfare agency. Christ did not call us to be a service provider; He called us to be servants. "For I have given you an example, that you should do as I have done to you."

Now, go do it!

www.ingramcontent.com/pod-product-compliance
Lightning Source LLC
Chambersburg PA
CBHW070614060426
42445CB00038B/1076